Extreme Office Crafts

Extreme Office Crafts

Creative & Devious Ways to Waste Office Supplies & Company Time

Jimmy Knight & Tom Chalmers

LARK BOOKS

A Division of Sterling Publishing Co., Inc.

New York

Cast of Characters

Joe Rhatigan
& Rose McLarney
EDITORS

Susan McBride
& Megan Kirby
ART DIRECTORS

Cindy LaBreacht
COVER DESIGNER

Keith Wright
& Steve Mann
PHOTOGRAPHERS

Michael Sloan
ILLUSTRATOR

Shannon Yokeley
ASSOCIATE ART DIRECTOR

Susan Kieffer
ASSOCIATE EDITOR

Delores Gosnell
EDITORIAL ASSISTANCE

Megan Cox
EDITORIAL INTERN

Models:
LORETTA BALL
KATIE HUMPHRIES
CANDICE KILGORE
JONATHAN LIM
MICHAEL MURPHY
MATT PADEN
WENDY WRIGHT
TERRY AYOUB
FERNANDO PINZON
ANNA BELLE PEEVEY
MHOTEP MCKINSEY
SCOTT THOMPSON
NATALIE MORNU
PHILLIP ANGLIN

Library of Congress Cataloging-in-Publication Data

Knight, Jimmy, 1964-
   Extreme office crafts : creative & devious ways to waste office supplies & company time / Jimmy Knight. -- 1st ed.
      p. cm.
   Includes index.
   ISBN 1-57990-868-3 (pbk.)
   1. Office practice--Humor. 2. Office management--Humor. I. Title.

   HF5547.5.K58 2006
   650.102'07--dc22

   2006017273

10 9 8 7 6 5 4 3 2 1

First Edition

Published by Lark Books, A Division of
Sterling Publishing Co., Inc.
387 Park Avenue South, New York, N.Y. 10016

Text and photography © 2006, Lark Books
Illustrations © 2006, Michael Sloan

Distributed in Canada by Sterling Publishing,
c/o Canadian Manda Group, 165 Dufferin Street
Toronto, Ontario, Canada M6K 3H6

Distributed in the United Kingdom by GMC Distribution Services,
Castle Place, 166 High Street, Lewes, East Sussex, England BN7 1XU

Distributed in Australia by Capricorn Link (Australia) Pty Ltd.,
P.O. Box 704, Windsor, NSW 2756 Australia

If you have questions or comments about this book, please contact:
Lark Books
67 Broadway
Asheville, NC 28801
(828) 253-0467

Manufactured in China

ISBN 13: 978-1-57990-868-3
ISBN 10: 1-57990-868-3

For information about custom editions, special sales, and premium and corporate purchases, please contact Sterling Special Sales Department at 800-805-5489 or specialsales@sterlingpub.com.

Contents

You're Going to Goof Off Anyway

Okay, so you have to sit in an office all day. Well, technically you don't have to, but the starting salary for lying on the living room couch all day in your pajamas is not very high. How will you pass the time? Studies show that today's employees are spending more and more billable hours on non-work-related pursuits. College basketball brackets, online dating, speed sudoku.... But if you're going to kill time, why not have something to show for it (other than a gambling problem, a cyber-stalker, and a really short pencil)?

Here's a thought: Why not make something? You've got all the materials you need at your fingertips, as long as

your fingers can fill out a requisition form or find their way to the supply closet. This book shows you how to take all your free time and your unlimited access to office supplies and turn out crafts. You'll be happy to hear that the instructions are simple to follow and do not assume any advanced skill level. (Face it: If you had any skills, you would have advanced farther in the company by now.)

So, make a project. Make another. Keep going until it's time to go home. Just be forewarned: We care about your boredom, but not so much about whether or not you keep your job.

Helpful Rating Guide

For ease of use, each project in this book is rated using one of the guides below:

On the Radar: What are your chances of getting noticed by coworkers, HR, and/or management?

Time Waster: How much time will this project take to complete? Will you have to miss meetings getting the project done?

Difficulty: How much brainpower will you need to complete the project? Will it feel too much like work?

You're Toast: How close are you to getting the axe?

At Your Desk

Your desk could be so much more interesting than it is. (Okay, it could be in a better office at a nicer job. But this is a craft book, not a prayer book.)

With a little effort and ingenuity, you can turn your drab, old desk from a workstation into more of a play station. Think about it: you spend eight hours a day at your desk. That's the same number of hours you spend in bed—often with the same result. You may not be in control of much at your job, but you can do what you like to your desk. Hey, it's the locker of your adult life!

Misery loves company, no matter what company you work for.

Dr. Do-Very-Little Critters

There's no need to be so lonely at your desk. Rub out boredom and isolation with these office pets. They even clean up after themselves.

Requisition This

Block erasers (lots)
T-pins, pushpins, map pins
Eraser caps

1 Pushpins work perfectly well, but map pins and T-pins make a more nimble animal. Though these kinds of pins may not be common, someone in your office has them.

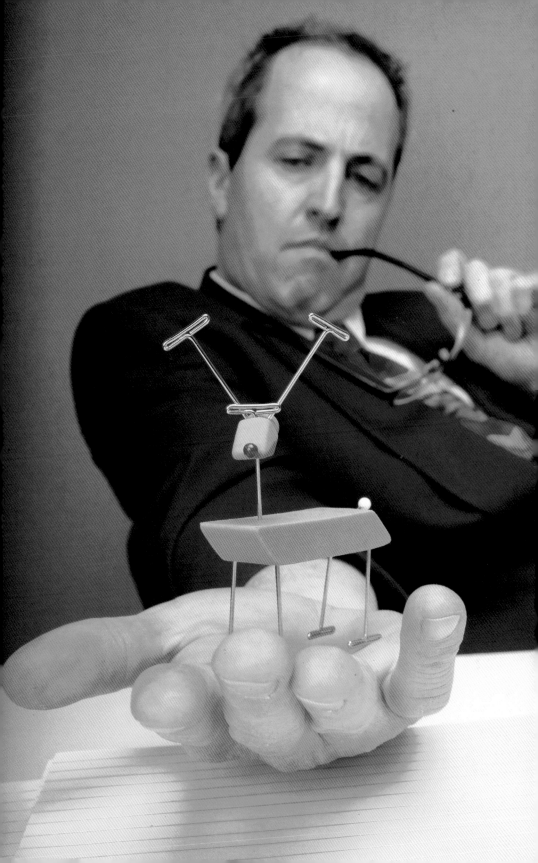

2 Use a block eraser for the body. To make an animal with long legs (antelope, elk, Doberman "pin-cher"), stick one T-pin in each of the four corners of the underside of the block eraser. Or, use pushpins to create a more compact creature (pig, pug, "porcu-pin").

3 To make the head and neck, run a T-pin through one side of an eraser cap and out the other. Stick the tip of the T-pin neck into the front of the top of the block eraser.

4 Stick the tips of two more T-pins into the top of the eraser cap head as antlers/antennae.

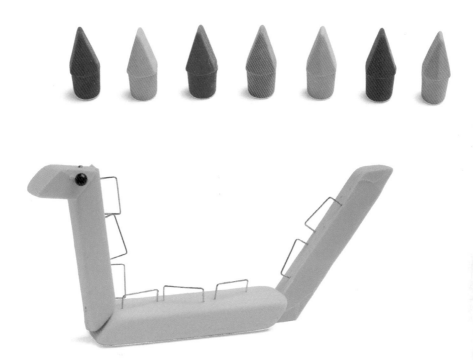

5 Map pins also make nice necks, antennae, and tails. Eraser caps make great snake heads. Incorporate additional office supplies for other assorted animals. Use scissors or a craft knife to cut up the erasers.

6 *If they ask about all those erasers: Explain that cleanliness is next to godliness. If you get any resistance, claim religious discrimination.*

These critters won't take up too much time—unless you're recreating Noah's Ark.

The latest in digit-al printing.
Thumb Print Art

Put your unique stamp on a masterpiece that is sure to receive at least two thumbs up.

Requisition This

Inkpads in various colors

Paper

Pens

1 Press your thumb, any finger, or a portion of your finger on an inkpad. Press your finger on a piece of paper.

2 Look for possibilities in the print. How about a turtle? Draw heads, legs, ears, whiskers, dots, designs, and other details around your prints.

3 *If they ask why your fingertips are inky: Tell them you've been cleared and all charges were dropped. Get instant street cred.*

No one should notice this fun little craft, unless your thumb art starts appearing on the quarterly reports.

Draw cartoons while
drawing a paycheck!

Card File Flip Book

**The only notable number in your
rotary card file is for the Chinese food
delivery place. Turn your laughable lack
of contacts into a funny flipbook.**

Requisition This

Rotary card file
Pen

1 Find a rotary card file to turn into
your flipbook. If you can't requisition one, take the new guy's. How
many numbers can he have?

2 Take out the dividers and cards.
Draw a cartoon action scene
frame by frame on the cards.
Use a separate card for each small
move or change.

3 Return the cards to the file in
their proper order. Spin the
wheel to animate your flipbook.
You can install several mini-flipbooks in
your card file. Reinsert the dividers
between them.

4 *If they ask why you keep flipping
through your card file with a smile
on your face: Tell them you're getting a contact high.*

Enjoy the light styles
of the rich and famous.

The Executive Tiffany Lamp

**Turn an ordinary desk lamp into a posh Tiffany lamp.
Give your desk a glowing sense of grandeur with the
transformational powers of file flags.**

Requisition This

Translucent file flags in assorted colors
Lamp with shade (if you don't have one,
bill one to your latest project)

1 What color is your cubicle?
Choose your file flags to match or
contrast. Also, it's best to work on
your lampshade with the light off,
unless you like having that green dot at
the center of your
vision. And, be sure to
make noise while
you assemble this
(peck on your
keyboard,
open and
close the occa-
sional drawer), so that
your boss doesn't think a
dark cubicle means you
have left for the day.

2 Starting at the
bottom edge
of the lamp-

shade, apply translucent file flags to create a border.

3 Apply a second row of flags,
aligning the bottom edges with
the tops of the previous row. To
create a checkered pattern, alternate
colors along the row.

4 Continue applying rows. You'll
find that you have to overlap the
flags' sides as you work your way
up a conical shade. If you have a cylin-
drical shade, you won't need to overlap
the edges.

5 Turn on the light, back up, and
bask in the stained-glass abun-
dance. Mr. Tiffany would be
proud, if he weren't busy being dead.

6 *If they ask why you need a lamp:
Claim a seasonal disorder. Why
you need so many file flags: Tell
them you suffer from O.C.D., obsessive
cataloging disorder.*

**The more obsessive compulsive you are, the better
(or worse—depending on how much you want to
keep your job).**

Eeeek, a mouse!

A Dead Mouse

Business is all about building a better mousetrap. But you already have a mouse sitting there on your desk. Quick! Kill it.

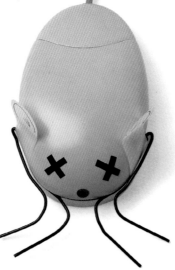

Requisition This

Computer mouse (You should probably use one that doesn't work anymore, since it definitely won't work when you're done with this project.)

Black tape

Scissors

Dot stickers (used for color-coding files)

Paper clips

File flags

1 The wire on the mouse will be the tail. The end opposite of the wire will be the face. Using black tape, make Xs on the face for eyes.

2 Use a dot sticker to make a nose.

3 Straighten out two paper clips. Fold each in half to make whiskers.

4 On each side of the face, run one paper clip through the grooves where the top piece of the mouse meets the bottom piece. This only works with some mouse models. So glue them on if you have to.

5 Cut two file flags into ears. Stick them to the sides of the head.

6 *If they ask why your mouse isn't attached to your computer anymore: Tell them you're trying to memorize all the key command shortcuts.*

This is an easy project. Explaining your actions to your coworkers, boss, and PETA is hard.

Know when to fold'em.
Inter-office Origami

So, you've received yet another memo about humming to yourself/smiling inappropriately at the interns/taking too long in the bathroom. Don't get discouraged. Repurpose these supposedly meaningful pieces of paper with the ancient art of origami.

Requisition This

Memos
....
Ruler
....
Pencil
....
Scissors
....

 To make your rectangular piece of paper square, follow illustrations 1 and 2 on page 95. The instructions on the right are for the crane. For anything else, simply type in "origami" in your web browser.

2 Fold the paper in half diagonally (illo. 1). Then, fold along the dotted line (illo. 2). Your paper should look like illo. 3.

3 Open the top flap (illo. 4), and flatten it to make a square (illo. 5).

 Turn over (illo. 6) and repeat (illo. 7). Crease the folds well. You should have a square (illo. 8).

5 Fold the upper flaps along the dotted lines (illo. 9). Turn over and repeat (illo. 10).

 Crease along the dotted line (illo. 11). Unfold (illo. 12).

 Bring the top upper flap down and fold along the crease (illo. 13).

 Turn over and do the same thing (illo. 14). Your crane should look like illo. 15.

9 Turn the crane body over (illo. 16) and fold the upper flaps along the dotted line (illo. 17). Turn over and repeat (illo. 18).

10 Open one of the side folds and bring the lower section to the inside of the body, folding along the fold line and ultimately, reversing the fold. Repeat with the other side fold (illo. 19). We sincerely hope your crane looks somewhat like ours.

11 For the beak, open one tip, and then push in to flatten and reverse the fold (illo. 20). Open the wings (illo. 21).

12 *If they ask if you have a copy of that important memo: Give them a choice of a crane or a dog.*

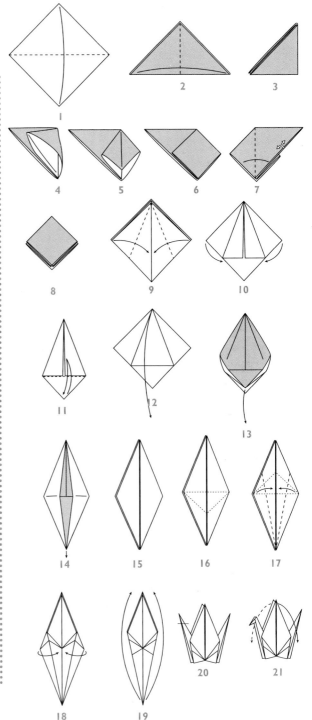

Origami can be challenging.
Paper cuts are a serious concern.

What's the point?
Pushpin Pointillism

Every office has plenty of pushpins. You could use them to post notices on new invoicing procedures. Or, you could grab a bunch and craft colorful creations like the ones you made when you were a hopeful, innocent kid.

Requisition This

Clip art designs (Eiffel tower, photo of New York skyline, etc.)

Printer

Bulletin board (11 x 17-inch boards work well, though we dare you to go bigger)

Carbon paper

Pen

Translucent, colored pushpins (lots and lots)

Ruler

Your thumb (or someone else's thumb, if they're willing)

1 Pick out a clip art design and enlarge it to the size of the bulletin board. You can orient your design either vertically or horizontally. Print it. (Of course, you may not need no stinkin' clip art design if it's all in your head.)

2 Place the carbon paper face down on the bulletin board. Put the design over the carbon paper, face up.

3 To transfer the design to the bulletin board, press down on the lines of the clip art with a pen. Remove the clip art and the carbon paper.

4 Using a ruler as a guide, insert a straight, evenly spaced line of pushpins in the bulletin board.

5 Following the carbon outline, fill in the central part of your design with rows of pushpins. Align each row, using the first row as a model.

6 After the central part of your design is complete, fill in around the design with pushpins.

7 *If they ask why you need so many pushpins: Tell them you're reading this great new "increase your productivity" book and you're on chapter one: Get Lots of Pushpins.*

 Don't push your luck.

For a real basket case.
The Totally Inbox

Does everyone dump all the work they don't want to do in your dumpy old inbox? Maybe if you upgraded it, the quality of the work would improve.

Requisition This

Large sheets of paper (preferably 11 x 17 inches)

Wire office basket

Ruler

Paper cutter

Scissors

Glue stick

Small binder clips

1 Find the largest sheets of paper you can. Rifle through wastebaskets near copiers and printers or raid your coworkers' "circular files" (a proud moment).

2 Count and measure the vertical openings between the wires in the bottom of the basket.

3 Use a paper cutter to cut paper into strips the same width as these openings. Make one strip for each opening. The box shown here used 14 1-inch-wide strips. But, the number of strips needed will vary depending on the design of your basket.

4 Weave the strips into the spaces between the vertical wires, one section at a time. Pass the paper over the first horizontal wire, under the second, over the third, and so on.

5 Once you've woven a strip through a section, fold the end to the inside of the basket, creating a flap. If the flap is more than ½ inch long, trim off the excess with scissors.

6 Glue the flap down. Repeat steps 4 and 5 for each strip.

7 Next, repeat the steps above, cutting paper strips to fit the spaces between the wires on the sides of the basket. Weave the back of the basket in the same way. Weave the front, using several shorter pieces on each side of the basket's opening.

8 *If they ask where your old inbox went: Tell them you're now outsourcing all your work. You're inbox is in India.*

It's difficult to hide your inbox. They always seem to know where to find it.

Whose Flowers?

Did some creepy guy send you flowers? Or, did a friend send you a bouquet for your birthday, forgetting how much you hate carnations? Don't pitch them, plant them. But not in the ground. Remove the card and put the flowers in a prominent position in the office. Watch as the unsolved mystery of who the flowers are for and who sent them eats up the entire office. For added drama, attach a card with the name smudged, signed "from your secret admirer."

Be the Picasso of partitioned walls.

Sticky Note Mosaic

**Tired of staring at that blank wall? Get the big picture!
Transform your cubicle from a mausoleum to a museum.**

1 Sketch out your design (favorite painting, pop culture icon, self-portrait) to get a general idea of where you will want to place the mosaic pieces.

2 Enlarge your design. (Trip to the copier!) Pin or tape it onto the wall or presentation board.

3 Start by filling in the main part of your design. Tear off the sticky portion of the sticky note, and then tear it into small squares. Place the squares on the design as you tear. If some pieces won't stick, just add glue to the back.

4 Then, fill in the background. It helps to start in the middle and work your way to the edge so you won't knock off pieces as you work.

5 Once you have the background finished, draw in the details with your trusty pen.

6 *If they ask why you need so many sticky notes: Tell them upper management has asked you to flag all the mistakes you find in your fellow employees' work. Watch how quickly they become cooperative.*

 Not only is it hard to hide a wall mosaic, but everyone is sure to tie your wall to the lack of sticky notes in the supply closet.

Cubicle Sweet Cubicle

The use of cubicles goes back to ancient times— it's just that they used to be called stalls. The fact that the inventor of cubicles also held a patent for an electronic tagging system for livestock makes the phrase "human resources" seem a tad suspicious, doesn't it? So, rise up, fellow workers! Reclaim your cubicle! Decorate! And we don't mean putting up pictures of some relative's kid who isn't really cute or a kitty calendar that reminds you to "just hang in there." Make your holding pen homey! Cozy up your corner! Pimp your partitioned party pad! Your cube shouldn't confine you; it should define you.

New friends from recent losses.

Quarterly Report Paper Dolls

While the company is cutting payroll, use your scissors to cut out companions for your cubicle. With a simple snip here and snip there, you can turn a string of disappointing earnings into a string of festive figures.

Requisition This

Print copy of the quarterly report

Glue or tape

Markers, pencils, highlighters

Scissors

1 Those big, boring reports printed on continuous feeding paper by accounting departments are ideal for this. (They are good for something other than a sleep aid after all.) But if you can't find continuous print outs, gather up a report on loose sheets of paper. Glue or tape the sheets together and fold them back and forth, accordion style.

2 Draw a gingerbread person figure on the top sheet, with one of the figure's hands and feet touching the fold.

3 Cut out the figure. Make sure you cut through all the pages but don't cut where the hands and feet meet the fold. Unfold the chain.

4 Use your markers to make these people in your image. Do they conform to the dress code? Remember, they're reversible.

5 *If they ask what you want with the quarterly reports: Tell them you want to peruse the reports for possible cuts in the budget.*

Depends on how scissor-happy you get.

OTB (Office Traffic Betting)

Nothing wastes time like placing wagers on random people walking by. I bet the next person who walks by will be wearing a bad toupee. I bet the next person who walks by will have toilet paper stuck to her shoe. I bet the next person who walks by will be carrying a carton of doughnuts (that he will eat all by himself). Play alone or with your next-door neighbor.

Stop and bend the flowers.

Paperclip Sculptures

If the only studio you go to is your one-room apartment, you can still get connected with your inner-artist.

Requisition This

Assorted paperclips

Needle nose pliers (see if you can get these from the maintenance guy)

Super glue

Assorted binder clips

1 Partially open a colored paperclip, pulling the small inner coil out so that the two ends of the wire touch. Repeat with three more paperclips of the same color.

2 Hook the four paperclips together in the center. Spread them out on a piece of scrap paper in the shape of a flower. Repeat step 1 with green paperclips to make leaves.

3 Straighten out another green paperclip for a stem. Put the top of the stem in the center of the flower shape and the bottom of the stem in the center of the leaves.

4 Place a large dot of glue over the center of the flower and the stem. Place a small dot of glue at the point where the stem meets the leaves. Let dry. Turn the flower over and put more glue on the back of the flower and stem. Let dry. Remove the tabs from a binder clip and stand the flower up in it.

If you start imagining yourself the toast of the town at little, mini art shows, it's time to alphabetize your files for a while.

No fourth wall? No privacy? No problem.
"Beaded" Curtain

Do you wish you didn't have such an open-door policy at your desk? Well, we have a swinging solution for you.

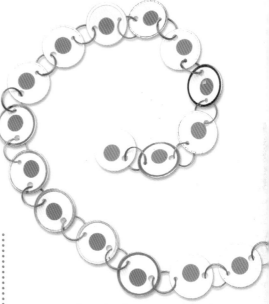

Requisition This

Dot stickers, many, many dot stickers
(used for color coding files)

Key tags with split rings (tons)

Single hole punch

Curtain rod ("borrow" one from
the lobby)

1 Do you just need a thin veil to protect you from prying eyes? Or do you crave a thick curtain to create a cubicle cave? Think carefully. Determine the size of your curtain and requisition, requisition, requisition.

2 Stick a dot on both sides of each key tag. Punch a hole at the bottom edge of each tag.

3 Join the tags by interlocking the split rings until you achieve the length you need. Make as many strands as it takes to provide the privacy you long for.

4 Place the strands on a curtain rod and let 'em hang.

5 *If they ask why you need so many key tags: Tell them you're running a bed and breakfast out of your cubicle to help make your numbers for this quarter.*

You might want to request comp. time for this one.

TIME WASTE-O-METER

31

Just mail this one in.

Padded Pillows

Late night? Do you feel like you're buried under a blanket of work? Don't lay your head on your desk. It can leave a mark. Make some pillows and put your troubles to rest.

Requisition This

¼ inch art tape (Settle for cutting some duct tape if you must.)

Scissors

White padded envelopes (assorted sizes)

Ruler

Shredded paper

Rubber bands

Hole punch

Glue

1 Cut and apply tape to the front of the envelope, making a fun design you're happy with.

2 To make fringe with art tape: Measure and cut 4-inch-long pieces of tape. Along the sides of the envelope, measure and mark points about 1 inch apart. At each point, place one end of a piece of tape ½ inch from the edge of the envelope. Turn it over and place the other end of the tape ½ inch from the edge of the back of the envelope. Press the tape down.

3 To make fringe with rubber bands: Punch holes every ¾ inch around the edge of the envelope. Run a rubber band through each hole. Then run the rubber band through itself and pull tight. Dab some glue inside the knot in each rubber band.

4 Stuff the envelope with the shredded paper and seal it shut for some shuteye.

5 *If they ask what you're mailing out in all those padded envelopes: Tell them it's certainly not your resume. That doesn't need any more padding.*

It depends on whether your pillows are used as decorative accents or for deep sleep.

Throw it in their faces.
Memo Face Clamps

Here's a creative way to interact with your fellow employees without actually having to talk to them.

Requisition This

2 x 3-inch color photo of a coworker's face

Scissors

Index card

Glue stick

Toothpick

Super glue

1¼ inch black metal clamp

2 inch black metal clamp

1 Cut out a coworker's face and glue it onto the index card. Cut out the face again. Then cut the face in two, going from one side to the other through the center of the mouth.

2 Using the toothpick, apply glue to the upper lip of the 1¼ inch clamp, being careful not to get any glue on the area where the edges meet.

3 Press the bottom of the face photo onto the glue on the lower lip of the clamp, lining up the edges. Press the top of the head onto the glue on the upper lip of the clamp. When the clamp is opened, the mouth should separate. Let the glue dry with the photo portion of the clamp turned facedown (preferably not on top of something important).

4 Close the tabs on the 2-inch clamp so that they are touching. Slip the top of the 2-inch clamp's tabs over the bottom tab of the smaller clamp. The larger clamp's tabs should lay flat on the back of the smaller clamp (see photo on next page).

5 Glue the two clamps together in the position shown in the photo. Let dry.

6 If you have a message that you need to give to "that guy" or "girl with glasses," don't go over to them. Throw it in their "faces" and let them pick it up later when they pass by. Make a clip with your own mug, too. When someone has some- thing to say to you, you can tell "what's-his-name" where to stick it.

7 *If they ask what you want with all those color photos: Tell them you just want more face time with your coworkers.*

You might actually get points for implementing a new communication tool.

Disco Desk

Don't get hung up when you hit that proverbial corporate ceiling. Hang something from it. Go retro chic. What better way to endure a 40-hour work week than with a 70's disco ball?

Requisition This

26 cone-shaped paper cups from the water cooler

Scissors

File folder

Glue

String

1 Don't throw those paper cups away; sneak them back to your cubicle. Do this until you have around 26. That's plenty of time-consuming trips to the cooler. Or, just take them all at once. Much more efficient.

2 Cut a circle with about a 1-inch diameter out of a file folder. This will be the base for your sphere.

3 Lay about eight cups around the circle on their sides with their tips in the middle. Glue the cup tips to the base. Fill in another layer on top with at least five cups. Point their tips toward the middle of the paper circle as well. Glue them down. You should have a half sphere.

4 Repeat steps 2 and 3 and build another half sphere. That's a "hemisphere" for all you geography buffs out there.

5 Tape a length of string or thread to the base of one half sphere. Glue the halves together. Let dry.

6 Hang the spheroid. To complete the discothèque effect, simulate a strobe light by quickly blinking your eyes over and over and over.

7 *If they ask why you need so many water cups: Tell them knowledge isn't the only thing you've got a thirst for.*

The project is not time consuming, but if you drink all that water, multiple trips to the bathroom need to be factored in.

Case the joint!
Jewel Case Tile Art

**Bored? Don't climb the walls. Cover them.
Turn your CD-burning habit into cool cubicle art.**

Requisition This

Clear CD jewel cases (lots of them)

3 packs of index cards, each a different color

Clear tape

Clear self-adhesive vinyl (intended for making labels or laminating)

Scissors

String, shoelaces, whatever

1 Remove paper or anything else in the CD cases. Arrange various colors of index cards inside. The placement is up to you. Be creative.

2 Arrange the cases, making sure every case touches the edge of another. Move the cases and adjust the colors until you're pleased with your design.

3 Tape the index cards in position. Close the cases. Cut a piece of the self-adhesive vinyl that is larger than your mosaic. Remove the paper backing from the vinyl and lay it sticky-side up.

4 Transfer your design, moving the cases onto the vinyl one at a time. Make sure you're placing the backs of the cases on the sticky stuff.

5 Cut the overhanging vinyl from around the edges of the cases. Stick any leftover vinyl on the back for extra reinforcement. Tape string to the back and hang it.

6 *If they ask what you did with all those jewel cases: Tell them you put them in a pirate chest and buried them at sea. Aargh! This is a lame joke, but a perfect opportunity to say "aargh."*

Hey, you're not wasting time, you're simply thinking outside the box.

Improve your outlook.

Window For Your
Windowless Cubicle

Don't spend another day staring at a padded partition.
Stare at a picture window (or a picture of a window) instead.

Requisition This

Clip art or stock photos of desired outdoor setting

Color printer

White poster board

2 wooden rulers

Glue stick

4 wooden yardsticks

2 paperclips

Box cutter (though a small handsaw would work better)

Super glue

Scissors

1 Enlarge the desired outdoor image so that you can print it out in four 8½ x 11-inch sections. Print it on the color printer using the poster function. (Of course, you can make your window any size you want.)

2 Place the sections of the photo on the poster board. Leave about 2 inches around the outer edges. Glue the sections in place.

3 The yardsticks will form the window frame running through the middle and around the image. To make the top and bottom part of the frame, cut two yardsticks off at about 21 inches. Assuming your office doesn't have a handsaw, you'll have to use the box cutter and really hack away at it. Be careful. This means you're going to have to exert a lot more effort during the workday than you usually do.

4 Cut the third yardstick into two 15-inch pieces to make sides. Cut the fourth yardstick off at about 18½ inches. This will be the horizontal bar running through the center of the window.

5 Cut two rulers off at about 6¾ inches to make the vertical bar through the center of the window. Fit one ruler piece on either side of the horizontal yardstick. Glue the pieces in position.

6 Cut off any excess poster board around the edges. For hangers, bend open two paperclips to form upside down U's. Glue them on the back of the poster board, in the upper corners, about 5 inches from each side. Let the glue dry.

7 *If they ask what you need with all those rulers: Tell them you're trying to measure up.*

This project is just slightly easier than actually boring a hole in your wall until you reach daylight.

Intercom Intrigue

If your office has an intercom system, take full advantage of the voice of authority. Disguise your voice and page yourself to various departments. "Please report to the mailroom… to the loading dock… to the Albany branch." Or really confuse your coworkers. Don't disguise your voice and page yourself to your desk. Get upset when you don't show. Get frustrated when you can't find you. This gimmick doesn't work as well if you don't have an intercom. You could try shouting, but they'll catch on quickly.

I-Tube.
Mailing Tube CD Rack

With all those annoying files and work-related forms cluttering up your cubicle, there's hardly any room left for your music library. Now you can stash your favorite CDs on a rack. Hook up to this tube for a musical life-support system.

Requisition This

4 inch x 43 inch cardboard mailing tube
(any big mailing tube will do)

Measuring tape

Pencil

Box cutter

1 Measure 6 inches from the bottom of the tube and make a mark.

2 Measure the thickness of four CDs. (This will vary depending on the type of CD case you have.) Measure the width of a case—usually about 5½ inches.

3 Draw a horizontal rectangle of this width and length, with the bottom edge at the 6-inch mark.

4 Carefully cut out the rectangle with the box cutter. The best way to do this is to run the cutter along the line several times, gradually cutting through. Remove the rectangle. Make sure your CDs fit snugly. Adjust as needed.

5 Measure up 2 inches from the top of the first rectangle.

6 Draw and cut a vertical rectangle that will hold five CDs. Continue adding alternating vertical and horizontal rectangular cut-outs along the length of the tube.

7 Try using smaller mailing tubes and creating a set of racks.

8 Is your rack wobbly? Well, don't expect everything to be perfect. Or, glue a large piece of flat cardboard on the bottom as a base. Heck, we're sure you can rig something up.

9 *If they ask when you're going to stop dancing and start working: Tell them you're gonna boogie oogie oogie till you just can't boogie no more.*

Relatively challenging, but not nearly as annoying as having to listen to your phone ring all day.

You Deserve a Break

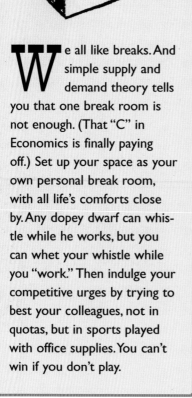

We all like breaks. And simple supply and demand theory tells you that one break room is not enough. (That "C" in Economics is finally paying off.) Set up your space as your own personal break room, with all life's comforts close by. Any dopey dwarf can whistle while he works, but you can whet your whistle while you "work." Then indulge your competitive urges by trying to best your colleagues, not in quotas, but in sports played with office supplies. You can't win if you don't play.

Your liquid assets.

Tavern on the Sly

Are you wasting away in a startlingly sober job situation? Raise the bar and secretly install it right over your desk. Now, with utmost ease, you can put all your drink fixings on the shelf, right next to your career ambitions.

Requisition This

Four 2-inch wide plastic binders
....
Ruler
....
Utility knife or box cuttter
....
Super glue
....
12 binder clips
....
2 metal bookends
....

1 Start by removing parts of the binders' covers with the utility knife. At about 8 inches from the edge, make a vertical cut all the way down the front of one of the binder's covers. An approximately 2-inch section of cover should remain attached to the spine. Repeat with a second binder.

2 Remove 8-inch sections of both the front and back cover from the remaining two binders.

3 Line the spines up side-by-side. Place the two binders with both covers removed in the middle of the row and an intact cover at each end.

4 Glue the cut covers together. Use binder clips to hold them in position until they dry. Waiting an hour or two should be a snap since you've been breathing in strong glue fumes.

5 Place a bookend at each end of the row of binders. Glue in place. Let dry. Place on the shelf. Stock mini-bar to your liking (preferably something top shelf).

6 *If they ask what is in those reference binders you are constantly consulting: Tell them you love numbers (singles, doubles) and every so often you just like to knock back a few.*

Your spiked drinks won't help with the spike in production that management is expecting from you.

Boss Cliché Bingo

Create your own bingo card by drawing a grid with six rows across and six rows down. But instead of filling the squares in with numbers, list all of the clichés your boss constantly spouts: Work smarter, not harder. Think outside the box. Love your job and your job will love you. Make several cards and hand them out to your coworkers.

Each time your boss offers one of his corporate catch phrases, mark it off. When someone fills in a row across, down or diagonally—BINGO!

Mind in the gutter?
Eraser Bowling

For now, your job is focused on the W-2 form and not the 7-10 split. But don't wait a whole week to get your bowling fix. Set up your own alley and roll away the hours.

Requisition This

10 eraser caps

Red pen

Red tape

Scissors

Ball from inside a computer mouse

1 Draw a red line around the tops of 10 eraser caps. These are your bowling pins.

2 Using the red tape, mark off an alley on your desk.

3 Set up the pins on the far end. Line up your ball at the other end and go for it.

4 Form a bowling league on your floor. Make your own trophies come tournament time (see page 29).

5 *If they ask why you've got all your coworkers shouting "strike": Tell them you're the new union captain.*

You should be able to fly under the radar unless you're wearing your bowling shirt and shoes.

Office Birthday Calendar

Make up a colorful calendar with the birthdays of everyone in the office on it. Don't bother to find out when people's birthdays actually are (that's too much like work). Just assign dates randomly. Why not give yourself several birthdays? Anonymously post in a prominent place.

Get your rah-rahs out.

Shredded Paper Pom-Poms

Root, root, root for the home office.

1 Separate the shredded paper into two equal piles. Even out the ends of one pile of paper. This will be your first pom-pom.

2 Loosely wrap a rubber band around one end to keep the shredded paper in place while you work. Measure 3 inches from the other end. Tightly wrap a rubber band around that point. Repeat, wrapping rubber bands below the first until they are ½ inch from the end.

3 Remove the first, loose rubber band that you put on and unfurl your pom-pom. Repeat step 2, using the remaining pile of shredded paper for your other pom-pom. Otherwise, you'd just have a pom.

4 *If they ask what you need with all that shredded paper: Tell them you're trying to be a cheerleader of industry.*

Requisition This

Handfuls of shredded paper

Rubber bands

Ruler

Secretly wired.
Computer Cafe

You're a java junkie, but the coffee in your break room is chock-full-of-nasty. Now you can store the high-end stuff under your desk where it will stay safe.

Requisition This

Dead or retired computer tower

Screwdriver (if needed to dismantle the computer)

Coffee and coffee related paraphernalia

Chocolate (for when you've had enough coffee)

1 Open the computer case, using the screwdriver if necessary. Remove anything taking up valuable storage space, such as all that silly archival information.

2 Stock the case with your favorite coffee and coffee products, or whatever form of caffeine keeps you awake.

3 Close your case and place it on or under your desk. Note: for additional camouflage, you may want to run a few cables from the tower to the underside of your desk. This will give it the appearance of a viable piece of equipment. (If only the same could be said of you.)

4 *If they ask why you are hand writing your memos all of a sudden: Tell them your hard drive's roasted.*

With caffeine, your attention to detail may actually increase. Yet another reason not to drink too much coffee.

Fore!
Mouse Ball Miniature Golf

Do you wish you were on the back 9, instead of working 9 to 5? If you can't get to the golf course (mainly because it's Tuesday and you have to work), bring the golf course to the office.

Requisition This

Eraser

Brad

Ruler (preferably with a hole near one end)

Paperclip

Receipt spindles

Duct tape

Scissors

Construction paper

Sand (optional)

Ball from inside a computer mouse

White correction fluid

1 To make your putter or golf club: Push a brad through one end of the eraser. Put the brad through a hole at the bottom of the ruler. Open the brad's tabs. If the hole is too big to hold the brad, put a paperclip over the brad before opening its tabs.

2 The receipt spindles will be your holes. Use colored duct tape to create flags for the tops. Cut out patches of green construction paper to place around the bottoms of the spindles. Include openings in the middle for the ball to fall through. You could also use salt for sandpits.

3 Remove the ball from inside your mouse. Paint it with the correction fluid and let it dry.

4 Place the golf holes around your office, get your putter, line up your shot, and be the ball.

5 Get everyone on your floor involved to make a complete 18-hole course (including the 19th hole—see Tavern on the Sly on page 44).

6 *If they ask why you've covered the entire office with AstroTurf: Tell them that real grass is much too difficult to maintain.*

This is a tough one to hide. Go ahead and make an extra putter for your boss so he doesn't get teed off.

Why wait for happy hour?
Sneaky Book Safe

You shouldn't be discriminated against just because your version of a break is several sips of hard liquor between meetings. It's not like you drive a forklift for a living—the heaviest machinery you're going to be operating is the copy machine.

Requisition This

Hardcover book (not too precious)
....
Small flask
....
Pencil
....
Ruler
....
Cardboard (the back of a legal pad works well)
....
Utility knife
....

1 Open the book to a page about one-third of the way through. Place the flask in the center of the page. Trace around the flask with the pencil.

2 Place the piece of cardboard in the book about 1 inch below the page you traced on. When you cut, the cardboard will prevent you from slicing too far into the book.

3 Run the utility knife along the outside edge of the pencil line. When slicing out the pages,
make sure they are lined up so that the cut edges will be straight. (Because a sneaky drunk is not a sloppy drunk.) Carefully remove the cut-out pieces.

4 After cutting about ½ inch down, lift up all but the last cut page. Use that page as the stencil for the next group of pages and cut again.

5 Repeat this process as many times as needed, continuously trimming the corners. Keep checking to see how much farther you need to cut. You should be able to fully drop the flask in the cavity so that the book can close completely. Once you can do that, your project is done and your job is a lot more fun.

6 *If they ask why you're always reading: Tell them a mind is a terrible thing to waste (but a wonderful thing when wasted).*

Let's hold off on emptying the flask until you're done with the utility knife. Don't drink and craft.

Bathroom break.
Restroom Sign Makeover

Just because you have to dress like a corporate clone doesn't mean the restroom icons can't mix it up a bit.

MEN

HEADLINE®

Requisition This

Adhesive business-card magnets

Scrap paper

Scissors

Assorted, colored index cards

Black pen

String

Clear tape

1 Cut an adhesive business-card magnet into small squares. Peel the paper backing off the squares and attach them to each part of the figure.

2 Lay a piece of scrap paper on top of the figure. Rub the paper to make an impression of the figure's shape. Cut out the shape. This will be the pattern for the clothing.

3 Peel the paper off another sheet of business-card magnets and lay it sticky-side up. Place an index card on the magnet and rub. Cut off the excess card.

4 Trace the pattern on the card and draw your design inside the traced lines.

5 Cut out around the design. The magnets will hold the clothes on.

6 Try making gallows by taping together pieces of another magnet. Tie a loop at the end of a piece of string and attach it to the gallows for a noose.

7 *If they ask who put the paper doll duds on the potty doors: Ask them if they'd rather the restroom symbols be naked. For shame.*

Explaining why you're hanging around the wrong washroom door can get difficult.

Had enough of the three-ring-binder circus?

Circus Darts

Are the corporate clowns getting you down? Take the office bull's eye off your back and hang it on a door or wall.

Requisition This

Bubble wrap

Scissors

Paper

Dot stickers (used for color-coding files)

Tape

Drinking straws

Thumbtacks

1 Cut a circle out of bubble wrap. Cut a paper circle of the same size.

2 Using the spacing pattern of the bubbles, place various colors of dot stickers on the paper. Assign a point value to each color. Or write numbers on the dots. Tape the bubble wrap on top of the paper.

3 To make a dart, cut off about one-third of the length of a straw.

4 Tape a thumb-tack onto one end of the straw with the pointy end facing out.

5 Cut slits into the other end. Insert small pieces of paper into the slits. Make as many darts as you need.

6 Hang up the bubble dartboard on a door, a wall, or whatever else you don't mind putting holes in. Grab a dart and throw! Have several coworkers go at it, too, keeping track of scores.

7 You can make several sets of darts, each a different color, and have teams. Losers buy the next round. You may want to wait until after work to settle up. But, chances are, you won't.

8 *If they ask why there are all those tiny holes in the break room door: Tell them you had to shut it on a swarm of bees.*

You'll always be on the radar when projectiles are involved.

Rubber Band Ball Juggling

You already juggle a successful career, active social life, and rigorous exercise routine. Wait, we're thinking of someone else. Okay, so you don't juggle—yet. You can learn how while you wait for the rest of your life to fall into place.

Requisition This

Rubber bands, lots of them

1 Tie a rubber band into a knot. Continue tying it around itself until you have used up its entire length. (You could start with a ball of paper for the center, but purists would disapprove.)

2 Twist a second band around and around the knot until you can't twist it anymore. Continue adding rubber bands until you're satisfied, exhausted, or out of rubber bands. Distribute the rubber bands evenly so that the ball will be round.

3 Once you've made three rubber band balls, you're ready for a new challenge.

 Making the balls is a breeze. Whether you'll ever learn to juggle is still up in the air.

How to Juggle

1 Hold two balls (A & B) in your right hand and one ball (C) in your left hand.

2 When you throw the balls, throw them so that they follow a rainbow path. Throw the outermost ball (A) in your right hand to your left hand.

3 While ball A is in the air at the highest point of its rainbow path, throw ball C to your right hand. Catch A in your left hand.

4 Roll ball B to front of your right hand and throw it to your left. Catch C in your right hand.

5 When ball B as it the highest point of its path, throw ball A to your right hand. Catch B in your left hand. Got it?

6 *If they ask why you need so many rubber bands: Tell them you're trying to keep it all together.*

Throw yourself into your work.
Binder Ring Toss

Challenge your coworkers to some carnival fun and see who will be lord of the rings.

Paper bursts (used for marking sale merchandise, specials, etc.)

Marker

Receipt spindles

Binder rings

1 Write a number on a paper burst. This number indicates the number of points awarded for a successful toss. 10, 20, 50, 100 points—you choose.

2 Pierce the paper burst on the tip of the receipt spindle and push it down.

3 Repeat this with as many receipt spindles as you want, marking each with a different point value.

4 Place the spindles in various places on your desk, on the floor, in the main hallway, or wherever there's room to play.

5 Toss binder rings at the spindles, keeping score of your points. Play with several people. The person with the highest score gets to pick where to go to lunch.

6 *If they ask what that clanking sound coming from your cubicle is: Tell them you're just tossing some ideas around.*

Break out of your penalty box.

Canned Air Hockey

Set some goals for yourself (and your opponent)—and decompress at the same time.

Requisition This

Sticky notes

Meeting agenda

2 cans of canned air (used to clean the sandwich crumbs out of your keyboard)

1 Call off the two o'clock meeting and clear the conference table. Use sticky notes to mark goal lines. Crumple up the meeting agenda. (It's your puck.)

2 The canned air containers are your "sticks."

Press the trigger of the can and aim it at the puck. Make sure you keep the cans upright. Be careful, they can get really cold.

3 *If they ask why you're wasting so much air: Tell them you wouldn't want to be canned either.*

Explaining to the IT guy why you need yet another can of air can get challenging.

They're out there. And they could be coming this way.

The Cubicle Peer-Over Periscope

No matter how much you stare at your cubicle walls, you can't see through them, and standing is such a strain. But you don't have to abandon ship. Be the commander of your cube-marine.

Requisition This

2-inch round mailing tube

Utility knife

Ruler

Two 2-inch round mirrors (try mirrors from makeup compacts)

Duct tape or packing tape

Scissors

Mailing label

1 Remove and save the end caps from the mailing tube. Using the utility knife, cut a 2-inch circle at one end of the tube. Cut a second 2-inch circle at the other end of the tube, but on the opposite side from the first hole you cut.

2 Place one mirror inside the tube, facing up it at a 45-degree angle. Tape the mirror in position. Be careful not to cover too much of the mirror with tape. (See the illustration to get this right.)

3 Slide the second mirror into the other circle, also at a 45-degree angle. Line up the mirrors and tape the second mirror in place.

4 Replace the end caps. Make a fake shipping label and put it on the tube to disguise your periscope. Keep an elevated eye on your coworkers, and don't get caught. Dive! Dive! Dive!

5 *If they ask why you never seem to mail that tube: Tell them you're waiting for an address confirmation from the brig...um, boss.*

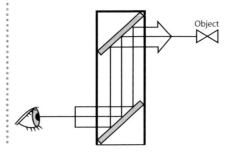

You'll be watching them, not visa versa.

Office Weapons

You toil in medieval work conditions, answering to an unsympathetic overlord. Don't languish in the Dark Ages. Outfit yourself with office equipment befitting the Knights of the Round Table.

T-square Crossbow

Requisition This

T-square

Tack dots

Rubber bands

Marker

Duct tape

Laser pointer

Binder clip

Eraser cap

Drinking straw

1 Place two tack dots on each end of the "T" of the T-square.

2 Stretch a rubber band over each end, and then pull the rubber band back as far as it will go. Mark this spot.

3 Using duct tape, attach a binder clip to the spot you marked.

4 Duct tape the laser pointer on the underside of the T-square, directly below the binder clip.

5 Pull the rubber band back and cock it in the binder clip.

6 Put an eraser cap on a drinking straw. Place the straw in front of the binder clip with the end of the straw touching the clip and the eraser pointing out.

7 Aim your crossbow, using the laser pointer for precision. Then release the trigger. Fly arrow, fly! Remember to crossbow responsibly. Don't aim at faces. And don't mess with building security. It's one thing to get fired; it's another to get fired back at.

8 *If they ask when they can expect those projections: Say you're sending them right over—via airmail.*

Chair Roulette

Call a meeting. Reserve a conference room. Fifteen minutes before the meeting, get a final tally of how many people are attending. Count the chairs in the room. Remove all unnecessary chairs, plus one, so you'll end up one chair short for the group. Hide the chairs you take out...hide them well. Take bets on who'll be standing up against the wall for the next hour.

Clipboard Crossbow

Requisition This

Clipboard
Thumbtacks
Rubber bands
Binder clips
Pencils
Eraser caps

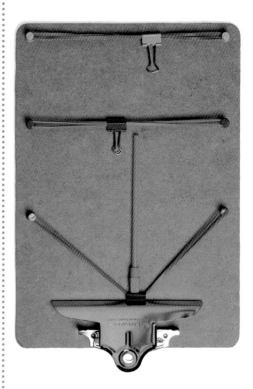

1 Insert one thumbtack on the side of the clipboard. Insert another on the other side, parallel to the first. Twist the thumbtacks to work them in. Most likely, the tacks will exit out the other end of the clipboard. Simply use the back of your tape dispenser or your stapler to hammer down those sharp points.

2 Stretch a rubber band horizontally between the thumbtacks. Attach a binder clip to the middle of the rubber band.

3 Holding the clip, pull the rubber band back until it reaches the clamp at the end of the clipboard. Clamp down on the lip of the clip.

4 Put an eraser cap on a pencil. This is your arrow.

5 Point the board at your target. Press the clipboard's clamp down. This will release the rubber band and clip. Watch your arrow fly! Try not to hit any upper management.

6 You have room on your clipboard to attach several rubber bands with different degrees of launching power. Place two more sets of rubber bands and thumbtacks on the board for short-, medium-, and long-range firing choices.

You're definitely going to be on the radar, unless you can take it out with your crossbow.

Make the best of the hand you were dealt.

Personalized Poker Set

When you got that big box of business cards, you felt like such a player. But now those cards are 999 reminders of your rotten luck. Turn them into a deck of playing cards, and remember, what happens in your cubicle, stays in your cubicle.

Requisition This

52 business cards

Dot stickers in four colors (used for color-coding files)

4 colored markers or pens (these should be the same 4 colors as the stickers)

Colored key tags

1 Use the dot stickers and markers to decorate the blank sides of the cards. For each of the four suits, you'll need cards for the numbers two through 10, a jack, a queen, a king, and an ace. Use different colors to represent different suits.

2 Put all the cards together facing the same way to form a full deck.

3 Remove the rings from colored key tags and use them as poker chips to place your bets (friendly or otherwise).

4 Shuffle the deck and deal.

5 *If they ask why you suddenly need more business cards: Tell them you're going to a convention… in Vegas.*

For once, you'll be playing with a full deck. However, it's not the kind of deck your supervisors were hoping for.

Looking Your Best with Office Supplies

Create your own cubicle couture. Requisition some exquisite additions to any wardrobe. They say that the clothes make the man, but in this case, the man (or woman) makes the clothes. This chapter also covers accessories, faux pas fixer uppers, and even safety wear. Looking your best was never so…strange.

Be **a model employee.**

Ravishing Binder Ring Belt

Stride down the hallway with glamour and clamor. Your bling-bling will go ching-ching.

Requisition This

Boxes of binder rings (in various sizes for added style)

1 Open one binder ring. Slip four rings on the open ring. Close the open ring. This is called a *chainlet*. Chainlet is a term from chain mail crafting. See, you're learning a valuable second language—unlike when you slept through those Japanese classes your boss sent you to.

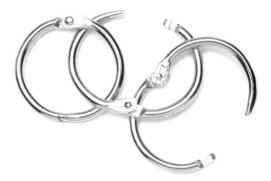

2 Make a lot of chainlets. Lay two chainlets down flat on your desk. Open a binder ring and join the two chainlets.

3 Continue linking chainlets until you have the length you desire. It should fit comfortably around your waist. (It's a belt, not a girdle.)

4 *If they ask where you got that fabulous new fashion statement: Tell them you found it in the back of the closet (the supply closet).*

Only the obsessive and daring have what it takes to requisition this many binder rings.

For when you pull an all-nighter.

The "Dirty Stay-Out" Kit

You and a few coworkers grab a drink after work. Sixteen unexplainable hours later, you're doing the walk of shame back to the office, wearing the same work clothes you had on yesterday. Don't be ashamed of your all-night outings. Just be prepared. Keep a "Dirty Stay-Out" Kit in your desk. The kit should include assorted items to disguise yesterday's duds.

- Stickers (dots and rectangles for labeling files, hole reinforcements, priority mail, etc.): Use stickers to give a plain tie an interesting pattern, a boring black skirt colorful accents, and a stained shirt a quick cover-up.

- Tape (duct, masking, clear, you name it): Strategically placed tape can alter the hem of a dress from below-the-knee to mini, give pants a stylish racing stripe, and even add professorial elbow patches on a sports coat.

- Markers, pens, and highlighters: Convert your generic garments into brand name apparel by drawing on the designer logo.

- Binder clips: Put your hair up any number of ways with these brassy barrettes.

- Glue stick: It's hair gel, with a strong hold.

- The kitchen sink: Throw in anything you can find that will make people say, "Don't you look nice today." And not, "What happened to you last night?"

Put your best face forward.

The "I'm Awake!" Snooze Master Mask

Thanks to this advance in slacker ingenuity, you can nod off yet appear not only awake, but alert. Just pop a sleeping pill, prop yourself up, and put on your game face.

Requisition This

Color, digital, close-up photo of your face

Access to color printer

Scissors

Cardboard (try the back of a legal pad)

Glue

Ruler

1 Get a friend to shoot a good close-up of your face with a digital camera. If you don't have any friends, ask a stranger. Send the file to your work e-mail.

2 Import the photo file to a friendly word processing or graphic program. Enlarge the photo to actual size. Keep trying different sizes and scales until you get a picture that is deceptively life-like. If it can fool you, it can fool them.

3 Print the image in color. (Black and white won't work unless you actually have a gray pallor to your skin and should consider seeking medical help.)

4 Carefully cut out the image. Cut out a slightly smaller piece of cardboard to use as backing.

5 Glue the photo and backing together. Glue the backing to a ruler. Leave several inches of the ruler extending beyond the bottom of the mask. You'll stick this part of the ruler down your shirt to hold the face up.

6 Find a safe pose and a good angle so that you're not easily detected. Pleasant dreams. Also available in "concerned," for when Janice stops by with updates on her sick cat, and "surprised," for when Neil tells his latest unlucky-in-love lament.

7 *If they ask why you're printing large, color images of your face: Tell them you want to be more of a presence in the company.*

You look raring to go. But be advised that snoring and drooling will blow your cover.

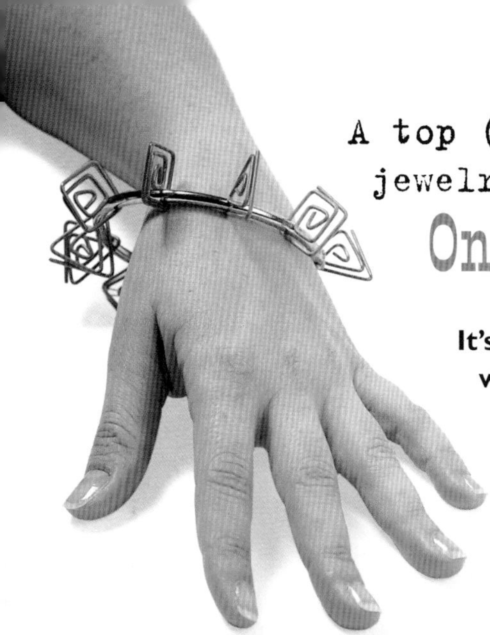

A top (desk) drawer jewelry collection.

On-the-Job Jewelry

It's hard to shine when you have to wear gray and office brown every day. However, you can add some sparkle by accessorizing the only place on your body not covered by the corporate costume: that small patch of skin between your fingertips and your cuff.

Requisition This

Various binder rings

Brads

Dot stickers (for color coding files)

Various paperclips

Rubber bands

Duct tape (in several colors, if possible)

Scissors

Markers

Emery board or metal file

Rings

Wrap a brad or two around a small binder ring. Stick a dot on top like a gemstone.

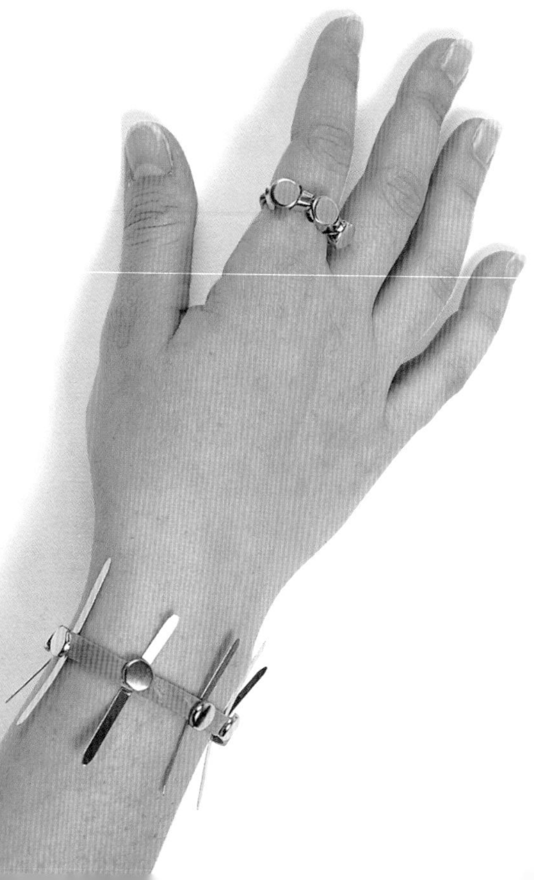

Bracelets

Thread paperclips onto a large binder ring for a dangly decoration. Or, punch brads through a rubber band and open them to make spikes.

Wrist Bands

Cut a piece of duct tape that's long enough to go around your wrist more than twice. Fold the tape in half, sticky sides together, and press it flat. (Sticky side out—ouch!) Decorate the surface with markers, brads, and cut pieces of tape of various colors. Punch holes in the ends, put brads in the holes, and use them to close the bracelet.

You should be okay, as long as you don't set up a sweatshop in your cube.

75

Forgot your tie? No problem.

Cork Tie

Your neck is on the line, and the last time you saw your tie, it was around your head while you sang "Don't Stop Believin'" at a karaoke bar. Use some bulletin board material that will help you look like you're boardroom material.

2 Decorate your tie with colored tape and dots.

3 Insert the cube clip into the back top of the cork tie (see photo below).

4 Clip the cube clip to your shirt and wear your tie.

5 *If they ask where you got that unusual tie: Tell them to cork it.*

Requisition This

Strip of cork

Paper

Pencil

Scissors or utility knife

Tape

Dot stickers (used for color-coding files)

Cubicle clip

1 Cut the cork strip into the shape of a tie. You may want to practice drawing the shape of a tie on piece of paper, tracing the shape onto the cork, and then cutting it out.

The tie's a little stiff, but so are your coworkers.

Dub yourself king or queen for the day.

Paperclip Crown

Use your mad crafting skills to usurp the position of emperor of the office. Amass and mold paperclips and let the coronation begin. Huzzah!

Requisition This

2-inch brass brads (lots)

2-inch brass paperclips (lots and lots)

Super glue

1½-inch round jewel-colored magnets

1 Spread the tabs of a brad open so that it lays flat. Slide a paperclip onto one of the open tabs. The inner coil of the paperclip should be on one side of the tab and the outer coil on the other side of the tab. Repeat with two or three more paperclips (see illustration below).

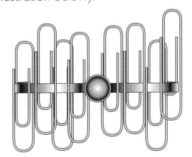

2 Slide three or four paperclips onto the second tab so that there are a total of eight paperclips on the brad. (Check out that illustration again.)

3 Fold the remaining portion of the brad tabs toward the back to hold the paperclips in place. Dab glue on the back on the areas where the paperclips touch the brad. Let the glue dry.

4 Open another brad. Weave one of the open tabs through the previously glued paperclips until the tab reaches the center. Fold over the end of the tab to attach the brad.

5 Using the technique described above, place three or four paperclips onto the brad's other tab. Again, glue the paperclips to the brad.

6 Keep creating these paperclip segments until you have enough to reach all the way around your head.

7 Weave the last tab into the beginning tab to form a circle and glue them together.

8 Glue on magnets, add spikes, and otherwise decorate your crown.

9 Assume the throne. Wave to the little people. Elbow, elbow, wrist, wrist, wrist.

10 *If they ask why you're wearing that crown: Tell them you wanted to put the "king" in the "kingdom," since they already have the "dumb" covered.*

Look, we did our best to explain how we made this particular crown. But use any way of hooking paperclips and brads together that you like.

Tired of being talked down to?
Stand Up To Your Boss Stilts

Is getting your supervisors to take you seriously a tall order? Give your confidence a much-needed boost with these nifty lifts. If you feel like you keep coming up short in the promotion department, rise up and demand that raise.

Requisition This

Reinforced packing tape

Scissors

2 large coffee cans with lids (found in most break rooms)

Ice pick or hammer and nail

Hole punch

Brads

1 To make the straps, cut two 12-inch strips of packing tape. Place the sticky sides together and press them firmly. We said firmly. That's better. Repeat to make the other strap.

2 On one side of a can near the sealed end, carefully punch two small holes using the ice pick or hammer and nail.

3 Using the hole punch, make two holes in one end of one strap at the same distance apart as the holes on the can. Attach the strap to the can with brads.

4 Put your foot on top of the can and pull the strap over your foot. Mark the spot on the tape where it comfortably meets the can. Not too tight! You don't want to give yourself blisters, do you? Punch two holes on the marked spots, then punch two holes in the can.

5 Fasten the strap with brads. Repeat with the second can.

6 For a slightly more subtle approach, put the plastic lids on the bottom of the cans before you go barging into the boss's office. Otherwise, you'll have the quiet grace of a horse on cobblestones.

7 *If they ask what the ice pick is for: Just mutter something about finally getting the recognition you deserve. They'll leave you alone.*

This shouldn't take up too much of your time, unless you can't find an ice pick or hammer and have to use your stapler or a lamp base instead.

Cover me, I'm going in!
Personal Haz-Mat Suit

Are you afraid to clean out the office fridge? Has Kevin in accounting's three-week-old tuna salad developed a heartbeat? Shield yourself from the science experiments your coworkers call leftovers with a three-piece plastic suit.

Requisition This

Bubble wrap (at least 18 inches wide)

Sewing pattern for hospital scrubs or other large fitting garments (check the internet)

Duct tape (safety color preferred)

Scissors

Marker

Measuring tape

Clear plastic folder

Clear packing tape

1 Lay the bubble wrap on top of the pattern. (All right, so you'll probably have to go out on your lunch break to get the pattern. But at least you'll be using tape instead of sewing.) If your sheets of bubble wrap aren't as wide as the pattern, tape the edges of several pieces together. Trace the pattern onto the wrap with a marker and cut out the pieces.

2 Tape the suit together following the pattern instructions. Or, wing it.

3 To make the helmet (and who doesn't love a helmet?), cut out two U-shaped pieces of bubble wrap. These pieces should be at least 18 × 18 inches each—large enough to envelop your head down to the shoulders. Tape the curved part of the two pieces together, leaving the straight edge open.

4 For the faceplate: Cut an elongated rectangular window out of one of the helmet pieces. Cut out a piece of a clear folder that's a little larger than the window. Tape the cut folder inside of the helmet window with the clear tape. Don't forget to come out for air.

5 *If they ask what in the world you're wearing: Tell the truth. Who wouldn't be happy that someone is finally willing to clean out the fridge?*

Fairly challenging and potentially noisy (Pop! Pop! Pop!). Warning: Do not wear Haz-Mat suit when gassy.

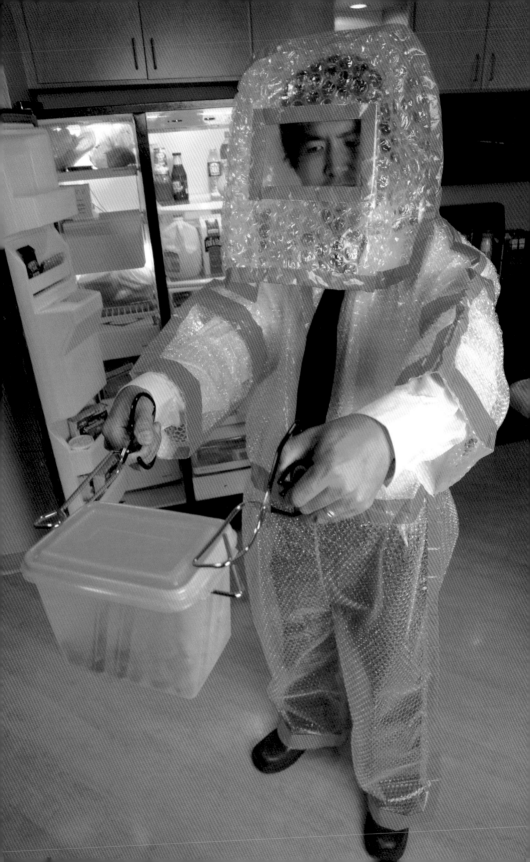

Dress snappy.
Rubber Band Suspenders

These elegant, elastic suspenders will help you keep your pants in place and your dignity intact.

Requisition This
Rubber bands in assorted colors
3 ID card holders with clips

1 To connect two rubber bands, thread one through the other. Hold both ends of one rubber band and pull down on the middle of the second until a knot forms between them.

2 Repeat, adding more rubber bands until you have a chain that is long enough to reach from your waistband, over your shoulder, to the center of your back.

3 Repeat steps 1 & 2 and make another chain like the first.

4 Attach the two chains at the point where they meet in the center of your back. To do this, run a rubber band through the end of each and knot it.

5 Make another small chain that will reach from the center of your back to your back waistband.

6 Knot this small chain to the point where you joined the longer chains.

7 Remove the plastic straps from the ID card holders. Run one strap through each of the three ends of the chains.

8 Clip two clips to the front of your waistband, to the back, and go. (Your pants are on, aren't they?)

9 *If they ask why you need so many rubber bands: Tell them you are trying to stretch your imagination.*

No one will notice—as long as you don't let one of the rubber bands go while tying them. They're dangerous when airborne.

Apply (to) yourself!
Ink Stamp Tattoos

C'mon, you know you've always wanted a tattoo. Now, there's a painless way to ink your arm. Instead of stamping bills as "past due," stamp yourself as a serious hardcore dude.

Requisition This

Block eraser

Pencil or pen

Utility knife

Inkpad

1 Draw the outline of a simple a design on the eraser. Using the knife, carve a shallow line just outside of your penciled outline. Then, cut along the inside of the outline.

2 Carve away the rest of the background material. Remember, only the raised areas of your stamp will get inked.

3 Press the stamp in ink and begin applying it—to yourself. If carving is too much trouble, just use the official stamps you already have. Who wouldn't want their forearm to say "paid"?

4 *If they ask if it hurt: Tell them no more than working here.*

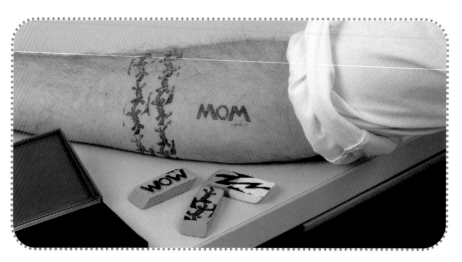

This project is a cinch. Having "Winona Forever" surgically removed is hard.

A quick end to a sticky situation.

Packing Tape Skirt

Brushed teeth? Check.
Portfolio for the big presentation? Check.
New shoes? Check.
Skirt? Uh oh.

Requisition This

Roll of 2-inch wide packing tape

Scissors

1 Um… start wrapping tape around your waist and work your way down. We hope you at least remembered pantyhose. Otherwise, ouch.

2 Wear it. Own it. And at the end of the day, simply peel it off.

3 *If they ask if your new skirt wears well: Tell them it can stand up to any-thing. (Hopefully you can, too, because you won't be sitting down anytime soon.)*

Making a skirt is easy.
Waxing with packing tape is painful.

Spreading the Joy

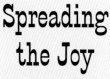

You've decked out your desk, improved your cube, and even upgraded your personal appearance. Don't stop now. It's time to share your gift of craft with the world, or at least the rest of the office. (It's either that or go back to work.) And for those times when you're forced to come out from your cubicle to celebrate some random calendar date with a group of people you don't particularly care for: lots of last-minute holiday ideas.

Bug your office.

Paperclip Office Pests

Assemble a swarm of bees, beetles, and centipedes and infest the office with them. Sit back and wait for the freak out. Or, if for some reason you don't wish to create a panic with your crafts, make adorable ladybugs and butterflies.

Requisition This

Assorted paperclips, fasteners, binder clips, erasers, pencil grips, plastic folders, pushpins, and anything else that looks like a bug part

Scissors

Glue

Permanent marker

1 Lay all of your assorted bug-making stuff out in front of you on the desk and start taking things apart and sticking things together. Mix and match materials to make an ugly bug, a sticky icky, a…you get the idea.

2 To make a centipede, hook three paperclips together end-to-end. Thread as many brads through the centers of the paperclips as possible. Open the brads' tabs. Attach a brad on each end and curl the tabs to create antennae. It's just not a bug without antennae.

3 To make a creepy crawler, use a pencil grip for a body. Stick push-pins in the head for the eyes and down the sides for legs.

4 To make a snail body, remove the tabs from the body of a curved binder clip. Save them for antennae; you can always use more antennae. Glue a geometric paperclip onto the curved clip for a head. Use two brads for eyes.

5 To make a ladybug, use a cubicle wall clip for a body. Glue on two spiral-shaped paperclips for antennae. Use permanent marker to make spots. More spots bring more good luck and waste more time.

6 To make a butterfly, cut a slit in each side of the pencil grip. Slide in paperclips and glue them in place. Glue on binder clip tabs for antennae. (See, we told you that you'd need them.) Glue a colorful pushpin on the end. Cut wings out of plastic folders and glue them to the clips on the side of the grip. Butterflies may be free, but your time isn't and you just got paid for putting wings on a pencil grip.

[x] 1–Unsatisfactory

JOB KNOWLEDGE
[Describe the level of knowledge that general. Rate his/her job knowl loyee studies accounting dge of where the atisfactory

[ ] 2–Satisfactory

[ ] 3–Averac

7 *If they ask where all these insects came from: Don't tell them the truth or they may exterminate you.*

Convincing the entomophobic to come back into the office may not be so easy.

The Mystery Sling

Show up to work one day wearing a sling. (If you don't have one, you can make one easily from an old pillowcase.) Chew up a good chunk of the day giving wild explanations as to what exactly happened: fended off a mugger, fell out of a moving car, had an unfortunate fondue accident, etc. For added fun, switch the sling back and forth from one arm to the other and see if anyone notices. You can get a similar effect with crutches or an eye patch.

Ears lookin' at you.

No-Brainer Holiday Headgear

The boss wants to see some holiday spirit ASAP. Show off your good attitude with a quick-like-a-bunny pair of holiday ears.

Requisition This

Wire coat hangers

Measuring tape or ruler

Wire cutters (ask maintenance)

Scrap paper

Pencil

Sheets of card stock in appropriate holiday colors

Scissors

Glue stick

1 Measure your head across the crown (from ear to ear) and cut a piece of coat hanger that length. At each end, bend the wire back about 1 inch so it won't stab you behind the ears. (You suffer enough at the holidays.)

2 Draw the design you want on scrap paper. Extending from the bottom of each drawing, draw a 2-inch tab. This will wrap around the headband. When you're happy with the design (and the design is happy with you), cut it out. This is your pattern.

3 Trace your pattern onto the card stock in pencil. Carefully cut it out.

4 Fold the tab at the bottom over the headband. Open it back up and place a line of glue across the inside of the fold. Lay the headband in position in the glue. Run more glue on the headband where the extra flap folds over and fold the piece shut. Let it dry flat.

5 Break out your special headgear for any occasion (including bad-hair days).

6 *If they ask why you're still wearing your ears days after Easter is over? Tell them you also celebrate Greek Orthodox Easter. Don't tell them you forgot to let the glue dry first.*

If you find that your head's hurting, it's not from thinking too hard. The wire's too tight.

Put your fingers in the future.

Corporate Cootie Catcher

It turns out that you did learn everything you need to know in the 4th grade. Reach into your past to give yourself the power to predict the future with a folded fortune-teller. Will you get that new job? What should you get for lunch? For questions as crucial as these, don't see a psychic; let this craft be your crystal ball.

Requisition This

Paper

4 colors of stickers

Black fine tip marker

Scissors

1 Fold one corner of the piece of paper to the edge to create a triangle (illo. 1).

2 Cut off the extra paper above the triangle. Open the paper and you will have a square (illo. 2).

3 Fold the corners together to crease an X in the paper.

4 Open the paper. Fold all the corners in to the center (illo. 3), creating a smaller square (illo. 4).

5 Flip the paper over so the fold-ed sides are face down. Once again, fold the corners toward the center diagonally (illo.5).

6 On the side you just folded in, write the numbers 1 through 8. Start in the upper left triangle and write two numbers per side.

7 Fold the paper in half. Open it. Turn the paper. Fold it in half again. Open it.

8 Under the numbers, there will be four flaps. Open each, one at a time, and write appropriate predictions. "You get the promotion." Or, "You find a dead mongoose in your desk." Fold the flaps closed (illo. 6).

9 Flip the paper over and place a different color of dot sticker on each of the four corners. Fold the paper in half (illo. 7).

10 Place your fingers under the flaps and work the paper upwards until you have the classic cootie catcher shape (illos. 8 and 9).

11 To use the fortune-teller, ask someone to choose one of the sticker colors. Open and close the catcher, moving from side to side, one time for each letter of the color they have chosen.

12 Then have the fortune seeker select one of the four visible, numbered flaps. Lift up the flap to reveal their fate.

13 *If they ask if these folded fortune-tellers really work: Tell them there's no other way you could have known there would be a dead mongoose in their desk.*

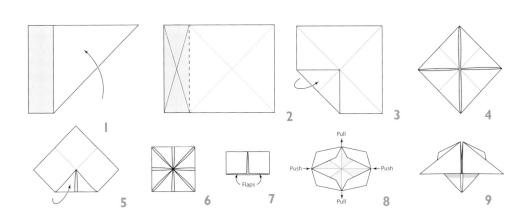

It's hard not to abuse the power of seeing the future (especially when you get to choose which possibilities to write down).

Unsuitable sales techniques.

Black Market Jacket

Do coworkers come to you for underground merchandise (pens, markers, whatever gets them highlighted)? Sport this coat and no one will suspect that you're the surreptitious supplier of sought-after office materials. Let all your regulars know that this traveling salesman now makes cubicle calls.

Requisition This

Large safety pins

Sport coat (preferably black)

ID card holder clips

Assorted office supplies

1 Pin safety pins in different positions on the inside of the sport coat.

2 Remove the plastic strips of ID card holder clips. Run them through the safety pins.

3 Attach assorted office supplies to the clips. Hang an open sign. Put a label gun in a pocket. (You're packing now.)

4 *If they ask why you always wear that same black jacket: Tell them black is the new black.*

Breaking a pack-of-pens-a-day habit is difficult.

Signs of the Times

Make restroom signs with symbols that have no discernible sexual characteristics. Watch as your coworkers try to figure out who goes in the ham sandwich door and who goes in the apple turnover door. Who goes in the starfish door and who goes in the mollusk door. Who goes in the question mark door and who goes in the exclamation point door. Whichever one they choose, walk in and say, "What're you doing in here?"

Go from corporate
puppet to puppet master.

Executive Puppetry Theater

Create a cast of characters from paper cups and put on performances to show your office mates what they missed at the morning meeting. Or, use these talking heads to tackle tricky situations like the always-awkward sexual harassment seminar. And puppets make firing a person more fun for everyone involved.

Requisition This

2 cone-shaped paper cups (from the water cooler) for each puppet
Markers
Pencil, newly sharpened
Brads

1 Curve your palm and lay a cup in it, seam side up. Use your other hand to gently flatten the cup out.

2 Pinch the tip flat. Curl up the sides slightly.

3 Repeat steps 1 and 2 with the second cup.

4 One cup is the face and the other is the lower jaw. When assembled, the seam sides are placed together and make up the inside of the mouth. Decorate the cups with markers. Make the puppet look like a person in the office.

5 Lay one cup on top of the other, facing in the same direction. About ½ inch of the bottom cup's corners should overlap the upper cup's corners.

6 With the pencil, poke a small hole through both cups at each corner. (No accidental piercings, please.)

7 Insert a brad and secure it by flattening the tabs in opposite directions. Repeat on the other side.

8 Operate the cups. Insert fingers and flap away.

9 *If they ask if a puppet is supposed to look like them: If they like it, take credit. If they are offended, deflect criticism by claiming that any resemblance to real persons is purely coincidental.*

Office reenactments have never been easier.

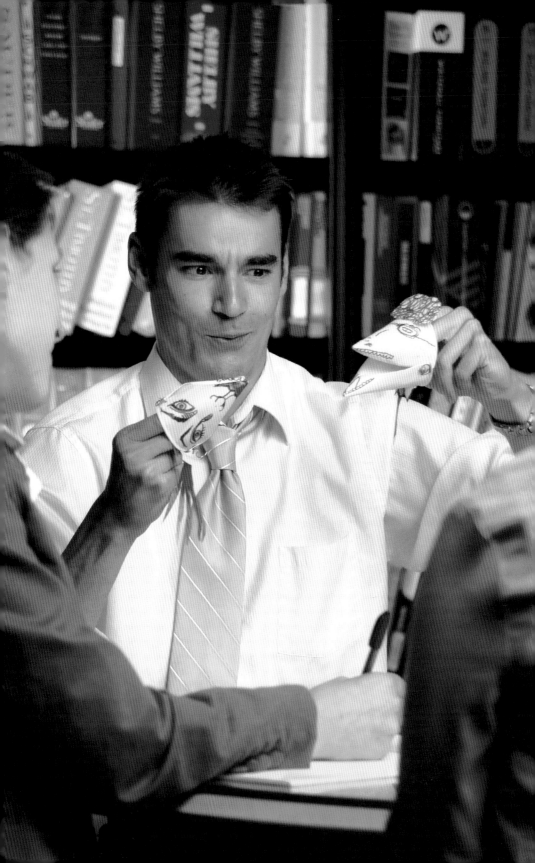

*When you care enough
to spend the very least.*

Crafty Greeting Cards

Is some random coworker celebrating a birthday? Is a fellow employee (who you couldn't pick out of a lineup) out with the flu? Don't spend your hard-earned money on someone you hardly know. Spend some company time and materials coming up with your own line of greeting cards.

Requisition This

Card stock or heavy paper folded in half to make cards

Various pieces of colored paper

Scissors

Colored staples (tell them they're no more expensive than the plain ones)

Stapler

Glue stick

Label maker with assorted colored tape

White glue

Glitter

Various stickers

Aspirin (or any medicinal items you can find)

Birthday card: Cut the shapes of a cake, candles, and flames out of various pieces of paper. Staple them together. Glue the cake onto a card. Add a message to the card with a label maker: "Wow are you old!" Apply dots of white glue and glitter as needed (and who doesn't need glue and glitter?).

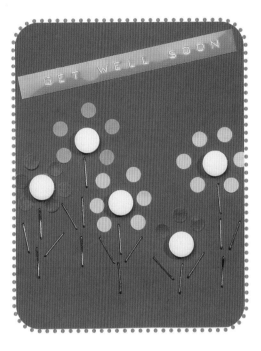

Get well card: Glue aspirin to the card for the centers of flowers. Place stickers around the aspirin to make petals. Use green staples to make stems and leaves. Add a label to the front of the card that wishes your coworker good health. Add a label to the inside that asks, "If you die, can I have your office?"

Bon Voyage: Staple the shape of the Eiffel Tower on a small, light-colored piece of paper. Glue the Eiffel Tower paper on a slightly larger piece of paper. Glue that paper on a card. Make a "Bon Voyage" label and place it above the staple tower.

If they ask where you get those great greeting cards: Tell them the cards benefit a charity. (Don't tell them that the charity is you.)

Real no-brainer. It's glue and colored staples, not quarks and black holes.

Scare up a scary outfit.

Hasty Halloween Costumes

The holiday that spooked you as kid is here to haunt you again. If you're expected to dress up and you forgot to get a costume, you can conjure one up. Sure, that awkward office party will still be an hour of your life you'll never get back, but at least it won't cost you a penny.

Accounting Tape Mummy

Requisition This

Accounting tape

Clear tape

1 Loosely wrap layers of accounting tape around and around your torso.

2 Using a separate piece of accounting tape for each part, wrap your arms, legs, and head.

3 Use clear tape to attach the loose ends to your torso.

stiff-legged rigor-mortis walk. But, some bandage breakage is inevitable.

4 Wrap a final layer around your torso. Add as many layers of paper tape as you can and work on your

5 *If they ask why you need so many rolls of accounting tape: Tell them that something just doesn't add up and you won't stop until it does.*

Spiral Binding Wig

Requisition This

50 12-inch black spiral binding coils

1 Select a spiral binding coil to be the center part in the hairpiece. Place a second coil at one end of the part coil at a 90-degree angle. Turn the second coil, winding it into the part until ¼ inch extends out of the opposite side. The spirals should hold together.

2 Using this method, continue attaching coils down both sides of the part.

3 Attach coils to one end of the part to be back of the hair. Leave the front end open.

4 Fill in the wig with the rest of the coils.

5 Try on the wig to check for gaps. Make adjustments.

Sticky Note Man

Requisition This

Sticky notes, loads of them

The party starts in four minutes and you're desperater than desperate. Simply stick a bunch of sticky notes on your clothes and go as the half-man/half-presentation known as Sticky Note Man.

These costumes take mere moments to make. Battling your arch nemesis Magnet Man is another story.

The &#!@% Hits the Fan

You knew this day was coming from the second you hesitantly accepted the position. As death is a part of life, getting fired is a part of getting a job. Maybe it's a decision you've been dreading. Or maybe it's an action you were actively campaigning for. (Many of the projects in this book are grounds for dismissal.) In either case, now it's time to take as many of their office products as possible. Just think of them as parting gifts from a really lame game show.

Getting nervous?
The Ancient Art of Binder Clip Acupressure

You don't need a medical degree to know that this job is killing you. It's a low, dull pain that starts as soon as you sit down at your desk and lasts until you clock out. The only remedy Western medicine can muster is retirement. But there is a way to relieve your pain and suffering by combining Eastern practices with ordinary office products. Grab a handful of binder clips and attach them to your hands, earlobes, and anywhere else you can reach. Alleviate the pressure by placing these pinchers on your pressure points. The Chinese have been doing it for over 5,000 years (that's a lot of lousy temp jobs). If nothing else, your coworkers will be so freaked out by your assorted attachments that they will avoid you all day. Peaceful isolation. You see, it's already working.

Have we mentioned that we're not responsible for any injuries, losses, and other damages that may result from the use of the information in this book?

Are the winds of change in the air?
Office Climate Gauges

Are you about to get blown off in a flurry of firings? These pencil-top pinwheels are not simple office toys; they're carefully calibrated instruments that predict the wacky weather patterns of the office environment.

Requisition This

Ruler

Pen

Assorted colored plastic folders

Scissors

Dime (don't worry, you get it back)

Straight pins (the ones with the little ball heads)

Colorful pencil with eraser

1 Measure and mark a 5-inch square on a plastic folder. Cut out the square.

2 Place the dime in the center and trace a circle around it.

3 Cut diagonally from one corner of the square toward the opposite corner, stopping when you reach the circle. Repeat at the other three corners.

4 Stick a straight pin through the center. Fold a corner down to the pin and, at ¼ inch from each tip, stick the corner on to the pin. Repeat with each corner.

5 Once the pin is going through all of the corners, push the pin and pinwheel—sorry, climate gauge—into the side of the lower portion of the pencil eraser. Leave enough space so the whirligig—err, gauge—sits loosely. The straight pin should not come out on the other side of the eraser. Now, if you sense a troubling downsizing trend, use your "brrr-ometer" to tell if the recent hiring freeze forecasts a cold front of cutbacks.

6 *If they ask about your new penchant for creating children's toys: Tell them to back off or the whirligig will predict their departure.*

Don't fold under the pressure of all that folding.

The ultimate "spell" check.
Do That Crazy Memo Voodoo That You Do

Oppressive memos, harassing notes, horrifying emails, and the most dreaded of all: poor performance reviews! If someone has crossed your inbox once too often, it's time to get busy and cure yourself of this scourge.

Requisition This

Memos

Stapler

Shredded top secret memos and pay-checks

Glue

Photo of boss

Map pins, other pins

1 Enlarge a particularly harsh memo from your boss. Print two copies on legal-size paper. Just to be spiteful, use expensive colored paper.

2 Place the two photocopied memos together. Fold them in half lengthwise. Now, cut out half of a human-like shape. Unfold the pieces, but keep them together.

3 Staple around the edges of the legs and stuff them lightly with some shredded memos. Staple around the torso and arms. Stuff them. Save the head for last.

4 If you'd like to personalize your voodoo doll, cut off—I mean, cut out—a picture of your boss' thick head. Glue it onto the head portion. If you can't find a photo (some demons don't show up on film), just draw a face.

5 Staple around the sides of the head leaving an opening on the top. Stuff the head and leave some shredded paper shooting through the scalp for hair (unless your boss is bald, then don't bother). Slowly staple the head shut. Admit it, that felt good, didn't it?

6 Prick, poke, and or stab the doll with a pin (scissors?) wherever the spirit moves you. Listen for the scream. Stick a new pin straight through any time you get another scathing memo.

7 *If they ask why you have a paper replica of the big guy: Tell them that men like him deserve to be idolized.*

Look, if you've made it this far through the book, your supervisors are pretty oblivious. However, if you get caught violently stabbing things in your work area, you will be led away.

Take more than your broken dreams with you.

False Bottom Box

They've told you to clean out your desk. So, why not clean out the supply closet while you're at it? Parting is such sweet sorrow, but it's particularly sweet when you can walk off with half the office.

Requisition This

Record storage box
2 record storage box lids
Masking tape
Negative reviews
Scissors
Rubber cement
White glue
Warm water
Cup
Pencil
Envelope moistening sponge

1 Construct the storage box and one lid. Tape the box together.

2 It's time to decorate your box. We're going to teach you the delicate craft of decoupage. (That's French for "gluing stuff to other stuff.") Pull out all of your negative reviews.

3 Use the rubber cement and attach the reviews to the box and lid, covering the entire surface.

4 Make decoupage glue by combining three parts white glue with one part warm water in a cup. Mix thoroughly with the pencil.

5 Using the envelope moistening sponge, paint the whole box with the decoupage glue. Wrinkles will disappear as the glue dries.

6 Create a false bottom by folding the second lid to fit inside the bottom of the box. Cut off any extra length on the lid. Insert the lid into the box with the top facing upwards to create an empty space underneath.

7 Store whatever secret severance parting gifts you gave yourself in this space. Place other items on top so that, should they check your box, it's all above board.

8 *If they ask why your pack-up box is so heavy: Tell them it's full of memories.*

If you had shown this much initiative while you were still working, none of this would be necessary.

Acknowledgments

A small band of people worked very hard to make this book of "craft" projects happen. Terry Taylor, Joan Morris, Steven James, Shannon Yokeley, and Susie Millions were the project designers who took a strange set of ideas and made them all come to life.

Susan McBride and Megan Kirby were brave enough to take on being the art directors. In addition to contributing valuable insight, they turned odd objects, frightening deadlines, and text into something that is funny and informative.

Photographers Keith Wright and Steve Mann made the process of shooting photography both professional and fun.

Many wickedly smart and talented folks at Lark Books contributed fabulous, twisted, cynical, evil, and outright brilliant ideas during the conceptual stages of the book: Joe Rhatigan, Bradley Norris, Dana Irwin, Jeff Hamilton, Linda Ragsdale, Joanne O'Sullivan, Matt Paden, Megan Cox, Megan Kirby, Nicole McConville, Rain Newcomb, Stacey Budge, Marthe Le Van and Veronika Gunter.

Special thanks to the management of the BB&T Building and Office Environments of Asheville, North Carolina, for their generosity and courtesy during the photo shoot.